The Louisiana Purchase

The Louisiana Purchase

Dennis Brindell Fradin

Marshall Cavendish
Benchmark

New York

Marshall Cavendish Benchmark
99 White Plains Road
Tarrytown, NY 10591
www.marshallcavendish.us

Text and map copyright © 2010 by Marshall Cavendish Corporation
Map on page 8 by XNR Productions

All Internet sites were available and accurate when sent to press.

Library of Congress Cataloging-in-Publication Data

Fradin, Dennis B.
The Louisiana Purchase / by Dennis Brindell Fradin.
p. cm. — (Turning points in U.S. history)
Summary: "Covers the Louisiana Purchase as a watershed event in U.S. history, influencing social,
economic, and political policies that shaped the nation's future"—Provided by publisher.
Includes bibliographical references and index.
ISBN 978-0-7614-4257-8
1. Louisiana Purchase—Juvenile literature. I. Title.
E333.F75 2010
973.4'6—dc22
2008036015

Photo Research by Connie Gardner
Cover Photo by Erich Lessing/Art Resource
Cover: The Louisiana Purchase document, with a map of New Orleans in the background
Title Page: A 1904 U.S. postage stamp commemorating the Louisiana Purchase

The photographs in this book are used by permission and through the courtesy of: *The Granger Collection*: 3, 29, 36; *Bridgeman Art Library*: The Arrival of
Englishmen in Virginia (coloured engraving), White, John, British Museum, London, 6; The Handful Who Conquered an Empire, Baraldi Severino, gouache
on paper, 9; John Hancock signs the American Declaration of Independence, 4th of July 1776 (colour litho), 12; Port of New Orleans engraved by D. G.
Thompson (coloured engraving) Waud Alfred, R. 20; Robert Livingston, 1804 (oil on canvas), Livingston (1654-1728), Vanderlyn, John c Collection of the NY
Historical Society USA, 22; *Alamy:* North Wind Picture Archives, 10, 34, 35, Classic Image, 24, 25; the London Archive, 26; *North Wind Picture Archives;* 11, 15;
Getty Images: Hulton Archive, 14; *Art Resource:* Erich Lessing, 16, Scala, 18; *Corbis:* Bettmann, 23, 42-43; *Corbis:* Bettmann, 23, 42-43; Connie Ricca, 32.

Timeline: Corbis: Bettmann

Editor: Deborah Grahame
Publisher: Michelle Bisson
Art Director: Anahid Hamparian
Printed in Malaysia
1 3 5 6 4 2

Contents

This colored engraving by John White, titled *The Arrival of the Englishmen* in *Virginia*, is displayed at the British Museum in London.

CHAPTER ONE

The Changing Map of North America

For many thousands of years, Native Americans had North America to themselves. By the 1600s, Europeans had begun taking over the continent. Three main countries colonized North America: Britain, Spain, and France.

Britain took control of what is now the East Coast of the United States. England established Virginia, its first American **colony**, in 1607. Georgia, Britain's thirteenth and last American colony, was founded in 1733. Britain's thirteen colonies occupied just a thin strip of land along the Atlantic Ocean, yet they were the seeds from which the United States grew.

Spain also claimed various parts of North America. Spain's North

area enlarged

Lake Huron

Lake Ontario

Lake Erie

(part of Massachusetts)

N.H.

NEW YORK

MASS. ○ Boston

CONN. R.I.

PENNSYLVANIA

○ New York

NEW JERSEY

Philadelphia ○

MD. ○ Greenwich

Annapolis ○

DEL.

VIRGINIA

Atlantic Ocean

NORTH CAROLINA

SOUTH CAROLINA ○ Wilmington

GEORGIA

N
W E
S

| 0 | 100 | 200 mi. |
| 0 | 100 | 200 km |

The original thirteen American colonies were settled between 1607 and 1733.

Legendary conqueror Hernando Cortés (1485–1547) is shown stepping ashore and encountering native people.

American **empire** included Mexico. It also included what is now the southwestern United States.

France was the third country that claimed North American lands. The French flag flew over Canada. France also claimed a vast area on both sides of the Mississippi River. The French called this region Louisiana for their king, Louis XIV.

Britain, France, and Spain waged wars to determine who would reign supreme in Europe. They argued and sometimes fought over control of the New World, too. For example, the French and Indian War broke out in 1754. On one side was France, along with its Native American and Spanish allies. On the other side was Britain, whose allies included its thirteen colonies and

Militiamen advance through the woods during the French and Indian War.

some Native Americans. In 1762, as thanks for Spain's help in the war, France gave the Spanish a gift: all of its Louisiana **territory** west of the Mississippi River.

The next year, 1763, Britain won the French and Indian War. As part of the peace **treaty**, France had to turn over all of its Louisiana territory east of the Mississippi River to Britain.

As a result, by the end of 1763 the map of what is now the United States had changed. Britain ruled most of the land east of the Mississippi River. Spain claimed most of the land west of the river. France no longer had a Louisiana territory—at least for the time being. Yet just a few years later, the map would change again.

These maps show land boundaries of North American possessions before (top) and after (bottom) the French and Indian War.

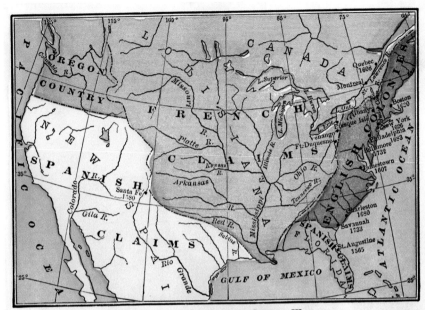

BEFORE THE FRENCH AND INDIAN WAR.

AFTER THE FRENCH AND INDIAN WAR.

Because John Hancock signed the Declaration of Independence first, his signature became famous. In fact, "John Hancock" has come to mean "signature."

CHAPTER THREE

The Dreams of Napoleon and Jefferson

In 1799 Napoleon Bonaparte seized power as France's ruler. Napoleon was a warlike leader with a large army at his command. His dream was to conquer the world. In 1800 he forced Spain to return the Louisiana Territory to France. By that time the territory consisted of a huge amount of land west of the Mississippi River. France did not do much to settle the Louisiana Territory and held it only loosely.

Meanwhile, in the United States, Thomas Jefferson was elected president in 1801. That year the United States celebrated its twenty-fifth birthday. The country had grown enormously in its first quarter century. For one thing, its population had more than doubled, from 2.5 million in 1776 to

"Mister Mammoth"

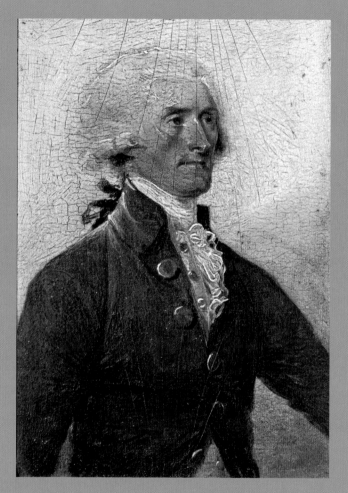

Thomas Jefferson (1743–1826) had a motto: "It is wonderful how much may be done if we are always doing." The tall, red-headed Virginian lived by these words. He was a lawyer. He wrote the Declaration of Independence. He served as the nation's vice president from 1797 to 1801 and as president from 1801 to 1809. He was a fine violinist. He was an **architect** who designed the Virginia state capitol in Richmond. Jefferson also founded the University of Virginia, invented a new kind of plow, and was called Mr. Mammoth because he collected **prehistoric** fossils. Thomas Jefferson lived to the age of eighty-three. He even died on a special day—July 4, 1826, the fiftieth anniversary of the Declaration of Independence.

5.5 million in 1801. Instead of thirteen states, there were now sixteen—Vermont, Kentucky, and Tennessee had joined the Union.

Also during that first quarter century, settlers had moved steadily westward. For example, by 1801 Alabama was home to more than 100,000 people. Ohio's population was about 50,000, while Mississippi's was around 10,000 and Indiana's about 7,000. These and many other territories east of the Mississippi River would become states in the first few decades of the nineteenth century.

What about the vast Louisiana Territory west of the Mississippi River? These were the lands France had reclaimed and now loosely held. President Jefferson dreamed of adding these lands to the United States, too. The Louisiana Territory was a place of mystery to Jefferson and other Americans. Its land, rivers, and mountains were unknown and unmapped. Many people told tall stories about the area. For example, it was said that some of the region's Native Americans were giants. Some people claimed the Louisiana Territory was the site of a nearly 200-mile-long (320-kilometer-long) mountain of pure salt!

President Jefferson wanted to explore the Louisiana Territory with the idea that the United States might one day own it. The problem was, France was not about to give the Louisiana Territory away. And the United States was in no position to tangle with Napoleon about it.

A view of the port of New Orleans. Founded by the French Mississippi Company in 1718, the city was under Spanish control from 1763 to 1801.

CHAPTER FOUR

Napoleon Takes a Bath

Upon becoming president, Thomas Jefferson appointed his friend Robert Livingston as U.S. minister to France. Jefferson sent Livingston to France on a mission. He was to try to buy the city and port of New Orleans from France for the United States. New Orleans was an important North American port for shipping. If the United States owned New Orleans, Americans could ship beef, flour, wood, and other goods down the Mississippi River to the city. From New Orleans the goods could be shipped to many other places.

Livingston arrived in France in late 1801. He met with two of Napoleon's top officials. One was the French minister of finance, François de Barbé-Marbois.

Livingston and the Louisiana Purchase

Robert Livingston (1747–1813) was born in New York City. He graduated from what is now Columbia University and became a well-known lawyer. Livingston was on the committee in the Continental Congress that created the Declaration of Independence. In 1789 he administered the oath of office when George Washington became the nation's first president. Livingston played a vital role in making the Louisiana Purchase. It is a little-known fact that he was hard of hearing. During the negotiations, the French probably had to yell in his ear to make themselves heard.

Talleyrand and Barbé-Marbois discuss points of the Louisiana Purchase with Napoleon.

The other was Charles Maurice de Talleyrand, minister of foreign affairs. Both took their orders directly from Napoleon.

Napoleon knew that the Americans would want more than just New Orleans. They would be pleased to own all of the French territory. At the time, Napoleon was planning to fight a war against England. Doing so would cost a fortune. Where would the money come from? Napoleon considered offering the United States all of the Louisiana Territory for a large sum of money.

He spoke to his officials about it. François de Barbé-Marbois said that selling the Louisiana Territory was a good idea. The United States or Britain might soon try to take the region by force anyway. Napoleon might as well sell the land and get something for it. Talleyrand disagreed. He insisted that France could build a mighty empire in its Louisiana Territory.

Napoleon leaned more and more toward selling the region. His brothers, Lucien and Joseph Bonaparte, heard about the possible sale. Like Talleyrand, they thought it best for France to keep the territory. One morning, in the spring

Lucien Bonaparte (1775–1840)

of 1803, Lucien and Joseph visited Napoleon at his palace in Paris. They walked in on their brother as he was taking a bath and advised him against selling Louisiana.

Napoleon grew angry with his brothers. "There will be no **debate**!" he said, meaning that his word was final. When his brothers continued to argue, Napoleon stood up in his bathtub and yelled at Lucien and Joseph. He was so furious that he fell back in the tub and splashed his brothers with water.

The argument with his brothers seems to have helped convince Napoleon to sell Louisiana to the Americans. Napoleon told his assistants to see what the Americans would offer not just for New Orleans but the entire Louisiana Territory.

Robert Livingston was still doing his best to obtain New Orleans for Jefferson. On April 11, 1803, Talleyrand invited Livingston to his office for a talk. Suddenly Talleyrand made a surprising remark. He said something like, "Would you Americans wish to have

Joseph Bonaparte (1768–1844)

the whole of Louisiana? I should like to know what you would give for the whole." This paved the way for what has been called the biggest real-estate deal in history.

Charles Maurice de Talleyrand (1754–1838) was an important diplomat but was not well liked by Napoleon.

CHAPTER FIVE

The Louisiana Purchase

After Talleyrand offered to sell the entire Louisiana Territory, Livingston was not sure how much to offer for it. He named a very low figure. The United States was willing to pay $4 million for the territory, Livingston said. As Livingston had expected, Talleyrand insisted that the Louisiana Territory was worth far more than that.

The next day, April 12, 1803, James Monroe arrived in Paris. President Jefferson had sent Monroe to France to help Livingston obtain New Orleans. Livingston told Monroe that he favored "making a push to buy the whole territory." Monroe agreed. He and Livingston planned their **strategy**. They expected the French to ask for a very large sum for the Louisiana Territory.

They would begin by offering a low figure. In the end, the two sides might meet somewhere in the middle.

Over the next several days, the two sides haggled. Livingston and Monroe **negotiated** for the United States. François de Barbé-Marbois was France's main negotiator. Barbé-Marbois began by saying that Napoleon wanted at least $20 million for the Louisiana Territory. The Americans countered with an offer of $8 million. That was not nearly enough, insisted Barbé-Marbois. He insisted that Napoleon's bottom price was $16 million. That was a little too steep for the United States, said Monroe and Livingston. However, they raised their offer to $12 million.

If the Americans could go a few million dollars higher, they would have a deal, said Barbé-Marbois. Finally, on April 30, the two Americans and the Frenchman reached an agreement. France would sell the Louisiana Territory to the United States for $15 million. Two days later, on May 2, 1803, the treaty was signed.

Livingston and Monroe were excited that the United States was gaining such a huge piece of land. As the deal was completed, Livingston declared, "This is the noblest work of our whole lives!"

In the early 1800s, there were no telegraphs or telephones. News traveled slowly between Europe and America by ship. Not until July 3, 1803, did news of the Louisiana Purchase treaty reach the White House in

Barbé-Marbois, Livingston, and Monroe signed the document on May 2, 1803.

"The Last of the Cocked Hats"

James Monroe (1758–1831) was born in Virginia and attended the College of William and Mary. He dropped out of college to fight in the Revolutionary War. Monroe took part in several battles and was wounded at the Battle of Trenton in New Jersey. Later he studied law under Thomas Jefferson, who once said, "Monroe is so honest that if you turned his soul inside out, there would be no spot upon it." James Monroe served as U.S. secretary of state and secretary of war. In fact, he held both posts at the same time. He was the fifth U.S. president from 1817 to 1825. President Monroe liked to wear old three-cornered hats from Revolutionary days. This gave rise to his nickname: the Last of the Cocked Hats.

Washington, D.C. President Jefferson was very happy about the news, which came one day before the nation's twenty-seventh birthday. The purchase was not official just yet, however.

According to the U.S. Constitution, a treaty could only take effect if two things happened. First, the president had to approve, which Jefferson did. Second, two-thirds of the Senate had to grant its approval. This was not so certain, for the United States had little money at the time. Some Americans thought that the country had no business spending $15 million for an unknown tract of land.

The Senate voted on the purchase on October 20, 1803. The vast majority of senators sided with President Jefferson. The Senate approved the treaty by a 24–7 vote. That was more than the two-thirds required to put the treaty into effect. The Louisiana Purchase was official.

This bronze relief sculpture, *The Signing of the Treaty*, was created by Karl Bitter for Missouri's St. Louis World's Fair in 1904.

CHAPTER SIX

A Turning Point

The United States had another problem. It did not have the money to pay for the Louisiana Purchase. The country had to borrow large sums from banks in England and the Netherlands. Since interest had to be paid on the loans, the U.S. government ended up spending much more than $15 million. The actual cost of the Louisiana Purchase wound up being about $23.2 million. This would equal about $500 million or half a billion dollars in today's money.

Still, the Louisiana Purchase turned out to be a fantastic deal for the United States. The country received 828,000 square miles (2,144,510 square km) of land west of the Mississippi River. For each square mile of land

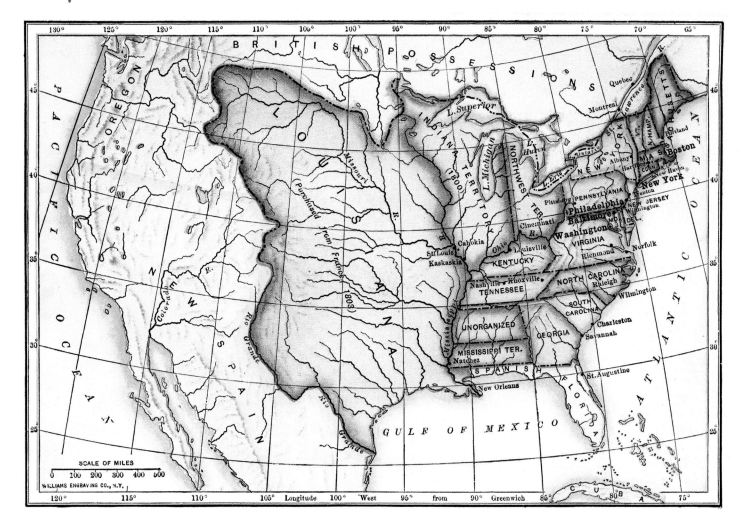

This map shows the large area of land that the United States gained as a result of the Louisiana Purchase.

gained, the government paid only about $30 in the money of the early 1800s. That was a low price, considering that eventually part or all of fifteen states were carved out of the territory: Louisiana, Arkansas, Missouri,

Wagons head West on the National Road, built with federal funds a few years after the treaty opened the territory to settlers.

Iowa, Minnesota, Texas, Oklahoma, Kansas, Nebraska, South Dakota, North Dakota, New Mexico, Colorado, Wyoming, and Montana.

Acquiring all this land was a turning point for the United States in several ways. The United States now had possession of New Orleans, as Jefferson had wanted. The young nation had gained vast lands for **pioneers** who

This painting shows a December 20, 1803, ceremony in New Orleans marking the Louisiana Purchase agreement.

The Emperor of France

Napoleon Bonaparte (1769–1821) was born on Corsica, an island that belonged to France at the time. He enrolled in a military school in France at the age of nine and joined the French army at sixteen. By the age of twenty-four he had risen to become a general.

Napoleon won battle after battle. He steadily gained power until he was crowned emperor of France in 1804. Although he was 5 feet 2 inches (1.57 meters) tall, Napoleon was strong and had an iron will. He sometimes worked eighteen straight hours. His empire eventually covered much of Europe. However, his army was finally crushed at Waterloo, in what is now Belgium. Ever since, people who fall from power due to a sudden, massive defeat are said to have "met their Waterloo."

wanted to settle west of the Mississippi River. This paved the way for tremendous numbers of settlers to come to the United States in the years that followed. In the deal, the young country acquired some rich farmlands. These **fertile** lands would feed America's growing population as well as people around the world.

Also, by doubling its size, the United States became a much stronger nation than it had been earlier. In fact, some historians believe that the Louisiana Purchase marked the start of the United States as a great world power.

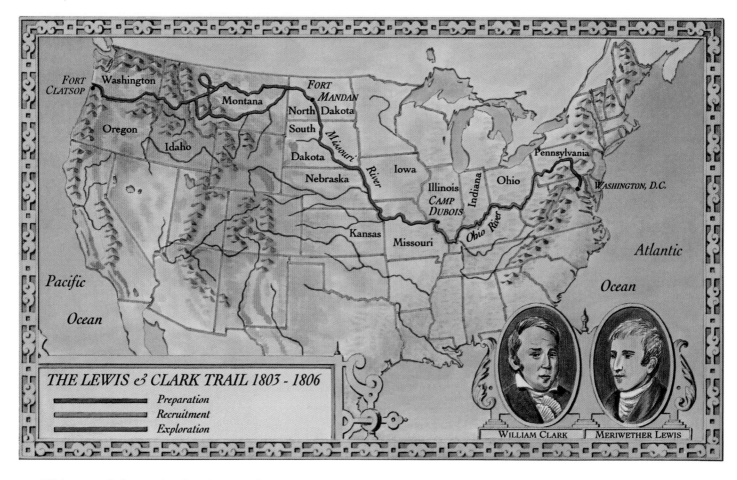

THE LEWIS & CLARK TRAIL 1803 - 1806

Preparation
Recruitment
Exploration

WILLIAM CLARK   MERIWETHER LEWIS

This map follows the Lewis and Clark Trail: the purple line traces the preparation, the green line, the recruitment of fellow explorers, and the red line, the exploration.

To the Native Americans, though, the Louisiana Purchase proved to be a sad turning point. When the French had held the territory, native peoples had been left alone for the most part. After the Americans took over, pioneers pushed the tribes off their lands, just as had happened on the East Coast.

What of the two leaders of their countries? Napoleon never achieved his dream of ruling the world. In 1815 the British and their allies smashed Napoleon's army at the Battle of Waterloo. Napoleon spent his last years imprisoned on the remote British island of St. Helena, in the South Atlantic.

President Thomas Jefferson, on the other hand, saw his dream of westward **expansion** fulfilled. In 1804 he sent Meriwether Lewis and William Clark to explore the Louisiana Purchase and other portions of the American West. The Lewis and Clark expedition paved the way for the United States to claim even more western lands. By the time Jefferson died on July 4, 1826—the nation's fiftieth birthday—the United States was on its way to extending "from sea to shining sea."

Glossary

architect—A person who designs buildings and other structures.

colony—A settlement that a country establishes outside of its own borders.

debate—An argument or discussion with two or more "sides."

empire—All the places and areas claimed by a country.

expansion—Growth or enlargement.

fertile—Rich; capable of being very productive.

independence—Freedom or self-government.

negotiated—Discussed with the purpose of making a deal or reaching an agreement.

pioneers—People who are among the first to move into a region.

prehistoric—Relating to a period before written history; extremely old.

strategy—A plan for a course of action.

territory—A region claimed by a country.

treaty—An agreement made between countries to establish peace or to cooperate in some way.

Timeline

1565—Spaniards found St. Augustine, Florida, the first permanent European town in what is now the United States

1607—England establishes Virginia, the first of its thirteen American colonies

1682—Frenchman La Salle explores the Mississippi River and claims vast territory for France

1707—England and Scotland unite to form Great Britain

1733—Britain founds Georgia, its thirteenth and last American colony

1754—The French and Indian War begins

1762—France grants all its Louisiana territory west of the Mississippi River to Spain

1763—Britain wins the French and Indian War; as part of the peace treaty, France turns over all its Louisiana territory east of the Mississippi River to Britain

1776—The United States declares independence from Britain

1607   *1733*   *1763*   *1776*

1783—With French and Spanish help, the Americans win the Revolutionary War; as part of the peace treaty, Britain grants most of its land east of the Mississippi River to the United States

1799—Napoleon Bonaparte seizes power as France's ruler

1800—Napoleon forces Spain to return its Louisiana territory—a huge amount of land west of the Mississippi River—to France

1801—Thomas Jefferson is elected third U.S. president; he encourages westward expansion

1803—Robert Livingston and James Monroe negotiate the Louisiana Purchase for the United States

1804–1806—President Jefferson sends the Lewis and Clark expedition to explore the Louisiana Purchase and other parts of the American West

1903—The United States celebrates the one-hundredth anniversary of the Louisiana Purchase

2003—The United States celebrates the two-hundredth anniversary of the Louisiana Purchase

1783 *1803* *2003*

Further Information

B O O K S

Nelson, Sheila. *Thomas Jefferson's America: The Louisiana Purchase 1800–1811*. Philadelphia: Mason Crest Publishers, 2005.

Schlaepfer, Gloria G. *The Louisiana Purchase*. New York: Franklin Watts, 2005.

Steele, Christy. *The Louisiana Purchase*. Milwaukee: World Almanac Library, 2005.

WEB SITES

For information about the Louisiana Purchase especially for kids:
http://www.socialstudiesforkids.com/articles/ushistory/louisianapur-
   chase.htm

For interesting information and pictures relating to the Louisiana Purchase:
http://lsm.crt.state.la.us/cabildo/cab4.htm

Bibliography

Blumberg, Rhoda. *What's the Deal? Jefferson, Napoleon, and the Louisiana Purchase.* Washington, D.C.: National Geographic Society, 1998.

Cerami, Charles A. *Jefferson's Great Gamble: The Remarkable Story of Jefferson, Napoleon and the Men Behind the Louisiana Purchase.* Naperville, IL: Sourcebooks, 2003.

Chidsey, Donald Barr. *Louisiana Purchase.* New York: Crown, 1972.

Fleming, Thomas. *The Louisiana Purchase.* Hoboken, NJ: John Wiley & Sons, 2003.

Keats, John. *Eminent Domain: The Louisiana Purchase and the Making of America.* New York: Charterhouse, 1973.

Kukla, Jon. *A Wilderness So Immense: The Louisiana Purchase and the Destiny of America.* New York: Knopf, 2003.

Index

Page numbers in **boldface** are illustrations.

About the Author

Dennis Fradin is the author of 150 books, some of them written with his wife, Judith Bloom Fradin. Their book for Clarion, *The Power of One: Daisy Bates and the Little Rock Nine*, was named a Golden Kite Honor Book. Another of Dennis's well-known books is *Let It Begin Here! Lexington & Concord: First Battles of the American Revolution*, published by Walker. Other recent books by the Fradins include *Jane Addams: Champion of Democracy* for Clarion and *5,000 Miles to Freedom: Ellen and William Craft's Flight from Slavery* for National Geographic Children's Books. Their current project for National Geographic is the *Witness to Disaster* series about natural disasters. *Turning Points in U.S. History* is Dennis's first series for Marshall Cavendish Benchmark. The Fradins have three grown children and five grandchildren.